TESTIMONIALS

'A very practical book covering critical aspects of leadership and the organisational culture that supports excellence. Lauren brings the lessons alive by weaving in personal stories which illustrate the points. A thoroughly good read.'

Rashid Kotwal, Revealed Resources

'Lauren gives plenty of great practical advice from her years of working with business owners, in a relaxed way that draws you from page to page.'

Paul Lindsay, Compass Assurance Services

'It provides good and relevant insights that are under pinned by stories to get the point across. I whole heartedly recommend this book.'

Barbara Sauter, Revealed Resources

'Having worked with many boards and executive managements teams in the not-for-profit space, Lauren's book is clear, concise and hugely helpful to guide and assist companies to get better period! It is something I intend to use.'

Christine Nicholls, Company Secretary

'Lauren Jones in her capacity as a consultant to my business for over 6 years now has enabled my business to put in place the mechanisms to grow my company and enrich my company. Since Lauren has been with us she has taken my company to the next level and looking beyond that as well. In reading this publication any business owner either large or small would be able to take something out of this book and apply to their business. The publication I believe takes away the complexity of issues and look at it in a different way.

I would recommend this book to any business looking to go to the next level.'

Greg Ingram, Managing Director, FNE Communications

10% Better

10% Better

Taking Organisations from Ordinary to Excellence

Lauren Jones

Contents

Ackowledgements

There is probably over 30 years of people to thank, as the ideas in this book have been formed from my whole experience of work and life, however it is important to acknowledge here the most recent contributors.

To be specific I would like to recognise Compass Assurance Services for needing me at just the right time; you triggered this journey. I am forever grateful, more than you can imagine.

There have been many organisations large and small who have allowed me into their fold over the past decade, and leaders who have entrusted me with their personal dreams and their teams' development. From you I have learned so much and am still learning.

For all the authors out there thank you. Reading your ideas and experiences helps to expand my thinking. Keep 'em coming!

Thanks to the team at Thought Leaders Business School who encouraged me to step up. This book is just one step.

To my support team who helped me make the leap, and who believe in me, thank goodness I found you.

And thanks to my family who are my reason for living.

About the Author

Lauren has spent over 20 years building her career in engineering, manufacturing, training, volunteering and consulting. She started as an electrical engineer in petrochemical manufacturing and quickly moved into operations management.

During that period the importance of quality assurance, health and safety, and environmental compliance became ingrained, while she developed important leadership skills heading an operations team. Developing management systems for ISO compliance and facilitating strategic objective setting workshops was a natural progression.

Lauren loves working with C level executives, business owners and leaders at all levels. She has seen terrific success with clients multiplying in size as she works with them facilitating their strategy, training their leaders, developing and refining their systems, and continuously improving their businesses.

What makes Lauren a little different is her deep understanding of how to turn compliance from a cost into a benefit. Her natural curiosity and experience make her realise there is a lot more than 'box ticking' to help clients improve their profit, processes, and productivity. As a trusted observer with a technical background, a good ear, a gentle 'sticky beak', a clear mind and talent for facilitation, she finds people listen to her and seek her counsel.

With decades of experience working with leaders of businesses, Lauren notices they are often-times in overwhelm, having to deal with change, cynical team leaders, lack of buy-in from staff without the measures in place to track productivity and success. Many are frustrated, dealing with internal conflict, and worrying about failure and the direction the company is taking.

Her **INSPIRE, EMPOWER and ENHANCE** suite of services help organisations keep focused and motivated on outcomes, their people aligned and skilled, their systems optimised, with metrics in place for feedback and conscious improvement.

It's about turning **Ordinary into Excellence**, and Lauren looks forward to working with you.

Who is this book for?

You could be forgiven for thinking this book is about productivity or continual improvement. It is true the word excellence has been 'stolen' from the manufacturing *operational excellence* terminology, but it is more than that.

This book is for business owners and senior leaders who are looking into the future at their organisation's longevity. It's for those leaders who wish to create an enduring legacy. It is also useful for compliance managers who are expected to influence both senior leadership and operational teams through the provision and implementation of management systems for their organisation.

In simple terms it provides a structure for your organisation to allow for sustainable growth and adaptability to change, thereby facilitating longevity by aiming to get 10% better.

Let's face it, the pace of change has accelerated greatly in recent years - the changing work environment, changing technology, changing supply chains and changing workforce expectations just to name a few. Futurists predict that the pace of change in the next 20 years will be 4x that of the past 20 years.

This book is for those who are time poor but love their work. It's for those who want to make a difference. It might even be for those who are a bit bored with the status quo.

And yes, it is for those looking to improve their profits year on year. If you could increase throughput by 10% or decrease waste by 10% or up productivity by 10% or reduce staff turnover by 10% or raise repeat customers by 10% … what would that do to your profits?

If you would like to achieve any of these, this book is for you.

Ordinary or Excellent?

- Are you working in an 'ordinary' business, following the market long after trends are established, or are you an Industry Leader?

- Have you just managed to survive the past couple of years, or have you been successful and profitable throughout?

- Would you describe your organisation as immature or refined?

- Are your people a little frustrated or are they empowered to make a difference?

  ____

- Is your company full of distracted individuals serving their own needs first or inspired teams who work together to achieve results bigger than themselves?

  ____

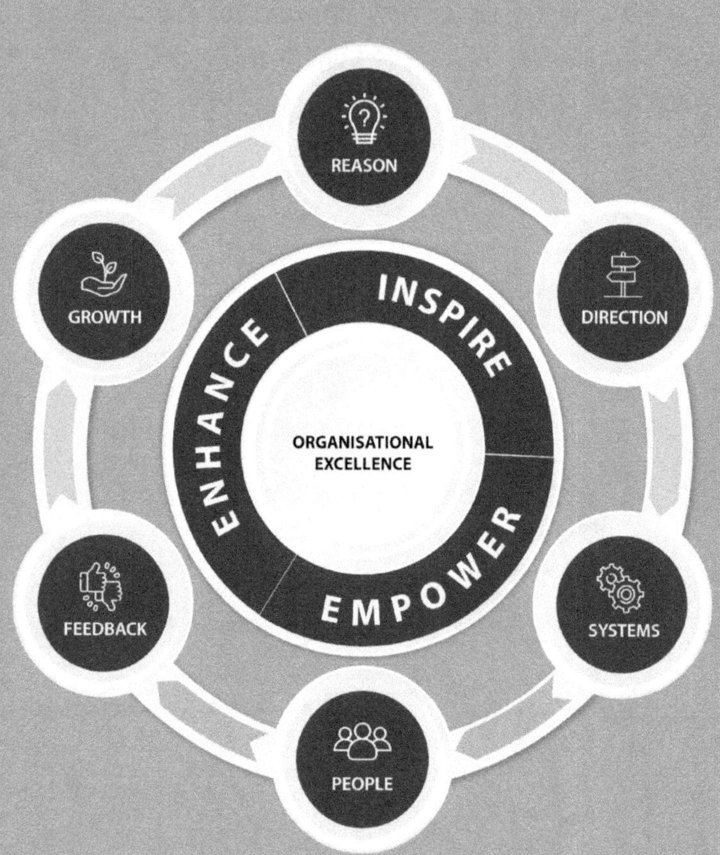

REASON
GROWTH
DIRECTION
INSPIRE
ENHANCE
EMPOWER
ORGANISATIONAL EXCELLENCE
FEEDBACK
SYSTEMS
PEOPLE

Introduction

"Corporate culture is the only sustainable competitive advantage... Develop a strong corporate culture first and foremost."

– David Cummings

Excellence is a Journey

The aim of this book is to help you set up your organisation for success. It's about embarking on a journey toward excellence; striving to be 10% better year after year by giving your business the best chance for longevity and your team the tools to expand and grow.

Many organisations have growth plans, but they lose their way. They focus on the wrong things and may not have the systems and processes in place that allow them to respond to the changing environment that they operate in.

With the increasing pace of change, an organisation that is here for the long term needs a strong identity combined with agility to deliver growth and excellence.

The Organisational Excellence wheel on the previous page illustrates the simple processes an organisation can put in place that will make the difference between an ordinary organisation and one that is striving for excellence. In the centre wheel I have simplified these into three focus areas or pillars for a company's management system. These are Inspire, Empower and Enhance, and each has a dedicated chapter within this book.

The outer wheel provides prompts for us as managers to help deliver the focus pillar. Put simply, to *inspire* we need a reason and direction, to *empower* we need good systems and desire to develop capability within our people, to *enhance* we need good feedback processes and a growth mindset.

Win the championship, not just the race

Over the past 30 years I have been blessed to work with a multitude of organisations of varying size, industry, pace and culture. What is very interesting is that a handful of them are quite satisfied with being ordinary, while a number are striving for excellence. Sitting in a third camp are those who have been operating with a level of excellence for some time. So what am I talking about when I refer to Organisational Excellence? I have struggled to find a definition I like so on the following page I have put it in my own words.

Notice the word continually. This means the organisation is able to deliver excellence through changing market conditions, staff turnover, introduction of new technologies, and all the other disruptions that are inevitable over the longer term. Which implies the organisation is continually adapting to change and consciously improving. Organisational Excellence is about longevity.

Organisational Excellence is a long-term approach to building an organisation that can sustain success and adapt to changes without losing its core focus. It is a play on the term operational excellence or Opex, which is well known in the manufacturing arena as the space for continual improvement programs, Lean Six Sigma and the like.

Organisational Excellence is when a company continually delights the customer through outstanding products and services, delights the employee through outstanding systems, processes and culture, and delights shareholders through outstanding results.

For much of the past decade I have worked in the compliance areas of quality, health and safety, and environment. Some of what I saw impressed and inspired me, but most frustrated and disappointed. I have attempted to illustrate these various company focuses in Figure 1.

It is a sad fact that many companies that focus purely on compliance tend to *stagnate*. Too many organisations put in a big effort before an audit, or perhaps for one customer or one project, but then let everything drop in between. An imposter, they might have moments once a year where everything is done perfectly, but frequently I have found these companies have set standards for the wrong reasons and those standards don't really serve the organisation.

By contrast, improvement-focused organisations may find themselves expending great efforts to fix whatever squeaky wheel is the loudest, but their efforts can be quite *inconsistent* because there is no external motivator for the improvement. They just 'fix' the issues when they come up. What they don't do well is anticipate their needs and embed these into their strategic planning and objective setting.

Organisations without a real focus on either is typical of start-ups. Because of their immaturity they would benefit from considering the culture they want to develop in the organisation in the long term. They are perfectly positioned to embed routine processes in the organisation to deliver excellence.

Ordinary organisations put in a big effort for one project or before an audit, but then let everything drop in between.

Don't settle for ordinary

Sadly, there are a lot of businesses who are settling on being *ordinary* because they think it is all too hard, or they are 'too busy' to be anything different. And they are one of the motivators for writing this book.

A balanced organisation that embeds risk-based decision making and continual improvement within its strategic planning activities - and uses compliance to enhance rather than constrict - will find it is able to build a culture of excellence that is continually looking to be 10% better. The result is an *resilient* organisation that can sustain change and challenge to achieve longevity and become a lasting legacy.

Organisational Focus

ORGANISATION	FOCUS
Resilient	Excellence
Adaptable	Understanding
Inconsistent	Improvement
Imposter	Compliance
Emerging	Ordinary

Figure 1

An example of poor attitude to compliance came from Volkswagen. Do you remember their vehicle emissions scandal?

In 2007 the EU introduced new rules for carmakers to prohibit so-called "defeat devices" – software that manipulated exhaust emissions depending on whether the car runs on a test stand or on the road. Yet Volkswagen continued to falsify their data and in 2014 a study conducted by the International Council on Clean Transportation (ICCT) revealed excessive emission volumes in several VW cars sold in the US. In 2015 the US Environmental Protection Agency (EPA) accused VW of installing illegal manipulation devices which they admitted to.

By 2017 a Volkswagen engineer and manager were both sentenced to time in prison, followed closely by the CEOs of VW and Audi (which was owned by Volkswagen).

Subsequently Germany also laid fraud charges, and countries such as Australia imposed significant fines on the company.

In November 2021 the High Court of Australia dismissed Volkswagen's attempt to overturn their $AU125 million fine for making false representations about compliance with Australia's diesel emission standards. In the US the company had already agreed to pay $US2.8 billion.

Fortune magazine (Oct 2020) reported that VW's cost of not complying was astronomical:

Volkswagen Cost of Non-compliance

 $billions in fines and other charges

 stock price plummeted

 30,000 jobs lost worldwide

 management charged with fraud

 untold brand damage

Figure 2

Not only when someone is looking

Unfortunately, the attitude of VW appears to have been "Compliance only when someone is looking". They wasted their energy designing software which made emissions acceptable, only long enough to fool the regulator, to then revert to non-compliant emissions for normal operation. If only they had expended that effort into improving the design, they would have saved billions and produced a better vehicle.

Dare I suggest that the culture of the organisation did not believe in compliance, yet it was their claim of compliance that allowed them to sell around 11 million cars worldwide, 57,000 of these in Australia.

Cost or benefit?

The VW story is a good demonstration of the cost of non-compliance, but is avoiding cost the only benefit? It is my belief that any compliance requirement should also be of benefit to the organisation, either by improving internal processes or external delivery or both. Implementation should ultimately reduce costs such as rework or recalls, reduce waste in resources and time, and improve sales.

Understanding the real costs is key to delivering benefits. Sadly, VW's focus was Compliance not Excellence.

In its simplest form Organisational Excellence requires leadership to establish a management structure with processes that deliver in 3 areas:

1. **Inspire your leaders**
2. **Empower your teams**
3. **Enhance your performance**

This structure has such depth to it that when followed you will find yourself building an organisational culture of excellence, and by embedding these processes into management cycles you will see improvements that may well exceed 10%.

Excellent organisations harness compliance requirements for the benefit of the operation, not for the auditor.

Online references:

1. https://business.linkedin.com/talent-solutions/global-talent-trends

2. https://www.afr.com/companies/energy/volkswagen-must-pay-record-125m-fine-for-emissions-scandal-20211112-p598f1

3. https://www.accc.gov.au/media-release/high-court-denies-volkswagen-leave-to-appeal-125-million-penalty#:~:text=Volkswagen%20admitted%20in%202019%20that,Government's%20Green%20Vehicle%-20Guide%20website.

Books mentioned:

1. Kurzweil, Ray 2005 – *Singularity Is Near: When Humans Transcend Biology*

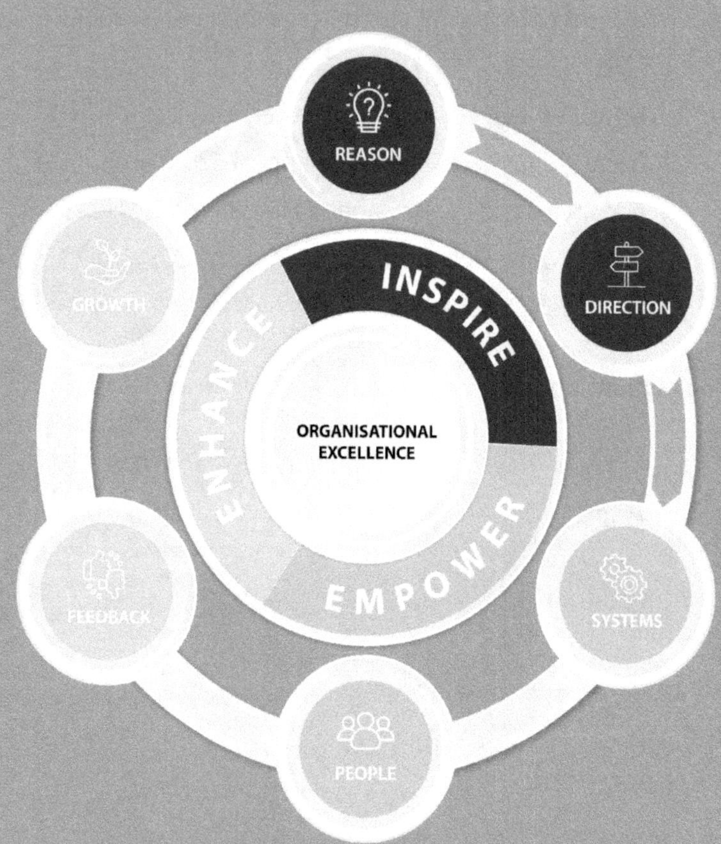
REASON
DIRECTION
GROWTH
INSPIRE
ENHANCE
EMPOWER
ORGANISATIONAL
EXCELLENCE
FEEDBACK
SYSTEMS
PEOPLE

Part 1

Inspire

"Unleash the potential that is in another and you unleash the potential that is in you."

– Matshona Dhliwayo

Your organisation is made up of people. This first section of the Organisational Excellence wheel is about the clarity you and your people need to ensure you are working together, working on the right things, and prioritising what matters to move forward. It's all about Inspiring yourself and your teams and operating better every year by making it part of your business cycle.

As a leader it is your job first to be inspired and then to inspire others. It is your role to define the vision for the organisation both in the long and short term and engage your team through a common purpose.

In the 2001 book *Good to Great*, Jim Collins talks about companies that reach and sustain greatness. They achieve this by finding what they can be the best at in the world, by understanding clearly where their profitability comes from, and they are deeply passionate about what they do.

Ordinary or Excellent?

- Do you know what you can be best at?

  ____

- Do you understand where your profitability comes from?

  ____

- Are you and the team deeply passionate about what you do?

The Bain & Company graph shared by Harvard Business Review and illustrated again here in Figure 3 indicates that inspired and engaged people tend to be significantly more productive than employees who are simply satisfied with their job and workplace.

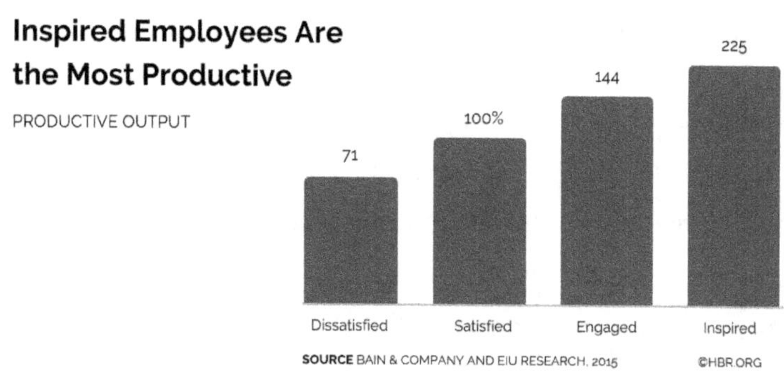

Figure 3

This is even more relevant now as we look forward to post pandemic ways of working, with high employment and the upheaval called the "great resignation" where employees are restless and seeking better conditions and more meaning in their work.

The most effective leaders will be looking to inspire and engage their teams through involvement in choosing the mountain they will climb and ensuring they share a common purpose or reason.

Reason

The first step on the Inspire segment of the wheel is to find your Reason. Teams will work more effectively if they have shared values and a common purpose. People need a better reason to turn up than just to get paid. Be clear on the reason behind everything the organisation does so that your teams can share common values and purpose.

"No company, small or large, can win over the long run without energized employees who believe in the mission and understand how to achieve it."

– Jack Welch

I play soccer. Actually I play in two teams, and what I've noticed in recent seasons is that the commitment to the team is very different in each case. One team is made up of middle-aged women who are "getting out for a run" with like-minded people. We're all Mums with varying commitment loads and turning up consistently on a Saturday is a challenge.

The other team plays Wednesday evenings. We're still middle-aged Mums (though the average age is a lot younger than me) but we are there to play seriously and to win matches. We turn up every week and never leave the team short.

In the first example, each player prioritises the individual over the team because their reason is about the individual not the team. In the second example players are committed to the team because we need the team to deliver a win.

No matter what people do, they will always have a reason.

In business the more the team share their reasons for being there, the more productive they will be.

Stick to Your Values

Values can make a significant difference to an organisation's results, and understanding the values as acceptable behaviours, provides clarity to leaders and employees alike.

Can everyone in an organisation really be passionate about what they do?

Having shared values and a clear purpose is one way that organisations generate passion. But a 2016 *Gallup* study showed that just 23% of U.S. employees strongly agreed that they can apply their organisation's values to their work every day, and only 27% strongly agreed that they "believe in" their organization's values.

Organisational psychologist Dr Kelly Windle talks about how culture is all about making and keeping promises. That sounds to me like building trust by being consistent with following through on what you say you're going to do.

Leaders' decisions and behaviours must consistently embody the company values so they permeate through the organisation, to the point where staff can also make decisions based on those values.

Values are a phrase, not just a word

Many organisations have a set of values, but are they meaningful and are they routinely tested? Describing a value as a phrase helps put much more meaning in a value than using a single word. Brene Brown, *Dare to Lead*, suggests new organisations should challenge the validity of their values after a year or two, and potentially do some tweaking to make the values more meaningful and useful. To be useful, values should guide decision making.

Older organisations may have had the same values for years, but through growth, acquisition, and general turnover, there may be a need to re-communicate the values with new staff.

How are values arrived at?

If you haven't established clear values in your organisation, your leadership team may choose to go through a process of discovery to capture the initial 'ideal' values. Then over time, challenge and refine these to the point where they will ignite passion and be enduring. This is often best done with an external facilitator and may be on a longer review cycle than other annual activities.

Have you ever played sport with an ace player who hogs the ball and scores all the goals by themselves? Over my years playing and coaching team sport I have experienced this on a few occasions. Sometimes the team loves it because that player is the difference between winning and losing. Other times the team hates it because they don't get to touch the ball.

Team values can vary

The team reaction depends on what the team values. Some value 'winning' more than they value 'team'. Neither is right or wrong, but the teams who don't clarify and align their values can encounter disparity and even discontent and lack of commitment.

It is the same for organisations. Leadership within the organisation who go through the process of understanding and defining organisational values are better equipped to make aligned decisions.

Turn values into behaviours

Brene Brown in *Dare to Lead* talks about taking this one step further by operationalising values into teachable and observable behaviours. Organisations that define example behaviours that either support or are counter to values, can use these to train employees and hold them accountable.

People trust leaders who are consistent, who stick to their values no matter who's listening. Being clear on your values can help you be consistent through those difficult situations and challenging moments that can arise in the workplace.

Are you clear?

Allow line challenges

There's no video ref in business. Or is there?

Do you remember the tennis player John MacEnroe who was renowned for challenging line calls? "It was on the line!" became the expression he was known for. The line challenge in tennis has changed dramatically with the invention of the Hawk-Eye System of using multiple cameras to track the ball and display a profile of its statistically most likely path as a moving image. The same technology is also used in cricket and football.

The professional tennis player can now challenge a line call and have a ruling made. In your business are players also able to challenge management? This can be as simple as encouraging discussion or through formal review of values and purpose on a set cycle.

Ordinary or Excellent?

- Does your executive team challenge each other in a healthy way?

  ____

- Do they challenge the organisation's values and purpose?

  ____

- How often does the CEO ask the team to challenge his/her decisions?

  ____

A Board of Directors can sometimes act as the video ref, observing from a 'helicopter view'. But the line challenge from the player who's on the court, holding the racquet, taking the shots, sweating it out, is equally important. They have the 'feel' of the game and the shot and know when a call doesn't feel right.

Have you challenged your values lately?

As an organisation grows and changes over time, it can be a beneficial exercise to revisit organisational values with the senior management team to re-align and 'operationalise' them.

For example, those managing recruitment should be hiring (and firing) based on those values, but if they are not part of the selection criteria then are those values really relevant?

Brene Brown (*Dare to Lead*) tells us that only 10% of companies actually operationalise their values. That is, they turn them into behaviours, train their people and hold them accountable. She goes on to say, that without taking the time to translate them from ideals into behaviours they might as well be on the wall as a cat poster!

Start with Why

Your organisational purpose is something bigger than just making money, and your people need to understand what that is to be passionate about it.

> *"Just as people cannot live without eating, so a business cannot live without profits. But most people don't live to eat, and neither must businesses live just to make profits."*
> – John Mackey, CEO of Whole Foods

Line Challenges from the Players are important.

In the 2001 classic book *Good to Great,* the author and his team of researchers studied a number of companies that moved from having good results to great results and managed to sustain them for 15 years. There were a number of findings as to how they did that, but Jim Collins suggests that at the core, is a clear understanding of what the organisation is about in figure 4:

Three Circles of the Hedgehog Concept

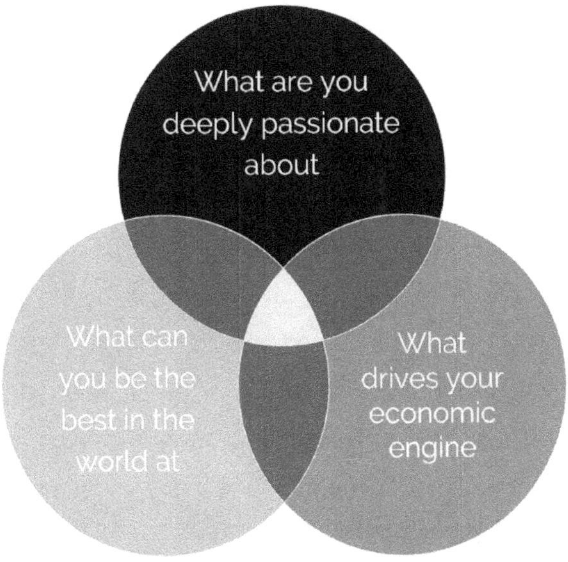

Figure 4

Understanding the answers to these 3 questions results in clarity of Purpose. The following story demonstrates how lack of clarity on our "why" lead to confusion and upheaval.

Some years ago, I had a leadership role with the local school band program. We ran a number of bands, with the senior band regularly achieving high standards at the various band festivals entered. The conductor for the senior band held the kids to high standards and the results showed.

Unfortunately, there were times where a child didn't want to attend rehearsal, citing that the conductor was mean and that rehearsal wasn't fun. There was one example I recall where a student was in tears during rehearsal.

As a parent committee we talked about our values and more specifically the purpose of the band program. Was it to teach children to love playing music by having fun or by winning medals at band festivals? Ideally it was both, but if we had to prioritise one or the other, we struggled. As the head of the committee, it was my responsibility to address this with the conductor, but I wasn't clear if there was a problem or not.

It took several attempts to decide on our 'why' and because we hadn't formally agreed and documented it, we were in-decisive for far too long

In the workplace, leaders need clarity to be able to have these difficult conversations. Does someone fit in? Do their decisions fit the values of the organisation? Do their behaviours deliver on our purpose? These conversations are never comfortable, and many leaders shy away from them, relegating them to HR or another manager, or not addressing the issue at all.

What's important in your organisation?

When approaching difficult conversations or making difficult decisions such as tendering for the next team project, it helps if you and your team fully understand the values and purpose of your organisation. When it comes down to it:

- Is it important to win awards?
- Do you prioritise being a family business?
- Is innovation or creativity essential?
- Are you keen to stay local? Or expand nationally?
- etc, etc.

Whatever your values and purpose, the clearer they are to you and your team, the easier it is to align your team's decisions and actions to them. Then if someone or some project just doesn't fit, those difficult conversations and decisions become easier. If we'd taken that approach with the school band program described above, it would have been much quicker and easier to decide what to do.

There's purpose ... then there's a greater purpose

A 2021 McKinsey report tells us that employees expect their jobs to bring a significant sense of purpose to their lives. Employers need to help meet this need or be prepared to lose talent to companies that will.

It's not just a case of a company purpose to make widgets and keep customers happy, it's also about contributing to society.

That's all wonderful and sounds easy if you're a big player with the capacity to have environmental teams and charity initiatives, but what about the small welding company in Newcastle? How does their work bring purpose to their lives? Interestingly, when I ran this exercise with that small welding business in early 2022, without prompting, their conversation was all around 'giving back'.

If they can, anyone can. Try stretching your purpose to include making a difference to the local community or perhaps the global environment and see how that feels.

This might sound in contrast to Jim Collins' teachings in his book *Good to Great,* where he suggests great organisations focus on what they can be great at and avoid getting distracted. This is where leaders sometimes become confused with a blurring between values and purpose.

Another 2022 McKinsey article talks about ESG (Environmental Social Governance) alignment with company purpose, stating that those with strong ESG records, performed better through the rising and falling markets of the pandemic. It refers to a Harvard study showing strong links between purposeful activity and productivity and performance improvements by engaged employees.

> *"We think about it as a grid with two axes. On one axis is whether you have strong or poor ESG performance and on the other is your purpose that sets your "North Star." You need to make sure that your ESG commitments deliver on the goals your purpose sets."*
>
> – Robin Nuttal

It's great to see the large, listed companies doing this. And it is also an opportunity for the smaller private organisations to follow suit.

Leaders, the key message here is to understand your values and purpose, then seek opportunity to contribute to 'the greater good'. A good facilitator will help you through the process, with the desired outcome for you and your team to have a clear understanding about what is important.

Direction

To be inspired and to inspire others also involves setting clear direction for the organisation, having strategy for growth and longevity, and ensuring that the teams share ownership of the actions required to get there.

It won't be long before we see autonomous vehicles stopping to pick up passengers and dropping them off again. But even driverless cars need information about their destination.

According to *Built-In* article in February 2022, 76% of employees believe that a well-defined business strategy helps cultivate a positive work culture.

In the movie 'King William', the father of Venus and Serena Williams had set a goal to have two champion tennis players. This goal was set before they were even born, and from the moment they were able to play they worked together on that plan. Even as young children they knew the direction they were heading.

Are you clear where the business is going and what steps need to be taken to get there?

Strategy

A well-designed strategy considers and responds to known risks, requires continual improvement and is delivered through quality objectives focused on enhancing customer satisfaction.

Understand risk

Before a rugby league State of Origin match, the teams analyse the opposition to identify threats and to look for any opportunity to take advantage of weakness. The teams also analyse themselves to identify their own potential weaknesses and to optimize their strengths. They have a winning attitude and as part of their preparation they ask "What could stop us?" to make sure they have planned for all potential risks.

In a similar way, Organisational Excellence requires analysis of self, the competition, and the environment in which you do business to understand internal strengths and weaknesses along with external threats and opportunities. Commonly used is a simple SWOT (Strengths, Weakness, Opportunities, Threats) analysis which can provide much insight to an organisation. However there are a myriad of tools available. PESTEL analysis is used to analyse the macro-environment focusing on Political, Economic, Social, Technological, Environmental and Legal factors. Culture and Stakeholder analysis may also be useful for understanding where an organisation stands before embarking on strategic thinking and risk planning.

Other tools can help determine the best strategy to choose. These can include cost/benefit analyses, decision matrices and risk registers.

Strategic risk tools help decision making

Strategic thinking tools are designed to help organisational leaders step back from the day-to-day activities to make informed decisions based on risk. The tools can help identify risks to guide the strategic planning process, and once you know where you want to go, they help identify "What could stop us getting there?"

As a leader, are you taking advantage of widely used thinking tools to ensure your planning and decisions are using risk-based thinking?

Draw your own map

Once your team understand their purpose and have identified potential risks, they need a plan or a map. This is a combination of long-term strategy and short-term tactics, which can be delivered through objectives and agreed actions. Try defining strategic priorities annually, based on current risks and gaps, before setting your objectives.

Are you strategic in your approach to setting objectives and goals, or are you a bit scrambled?

Take a look at the Priority Continuum illustrated in Figure 5 below. Write down where you think you and your immediate team sit on this Priority Continuum. Are priorities scrambled (no idea), are they spontaneous (let's focus on this now), are they strategic (long term, consistent). Are people divided and self-focused or are they united? Below are some definitions to help you decide what is your present Strategy Style? Are you above or below the line?

Priority Continuum

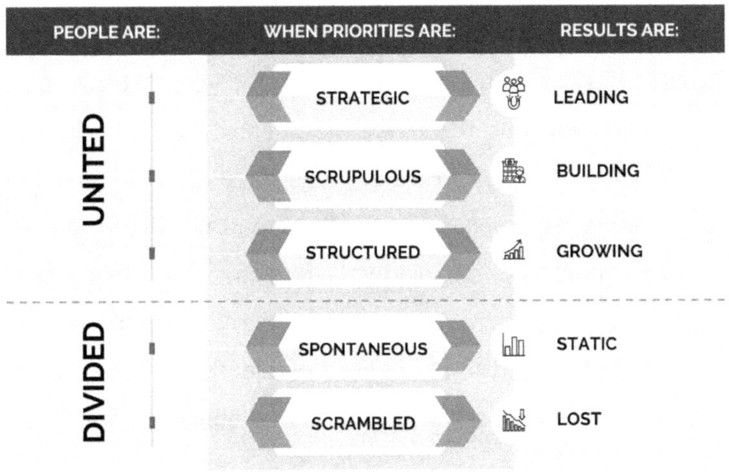

Figure 5

Scrambled: If you have no objectives your leadership/ management style could be described as Scrambled, and your people DIVIDED. Neither you, nor they, know what the priorities are so they become self-focussed and often times conflicting with their workmates or with your intentions for the business.

You need to start by defining goals or objectives to capture where you want the business direction to be set/focused for the next period. A period is often a year, but best considered when broken down into quarters.

Spontaneous: So you've set some goals but you still spontaneously react to the issues that arise each day. Your staff are dazed as they aren't aware of the objectives you've set, and they certainly haven't embraced them. It is vitally important to communicate the objectives to all team members at this point, so they understand the business priority.

Structured: When you start to be structured you are developing some priorities, but these are not necessarily followed up or relate to the bigger picture. If you have multiple teams or departments in the business, then the department/team leaders need to be empowered to clarify the objectives that are relevant to their team. For organisations as a whole, your employees will respond directly to the structure the objectives provide. Don't give up at this point, as you've just moved above the line.

Scrupulous: At this point you will start to be more scrupulous with how you spend your time. You and your team should regularly ask yourselves "Is this going to achieve my objective?" By utilising regular check-ins, team members will be driven in their approach and clear on priorities for their time and attention. There are various ways to conduct a check-in against your objectives, but I strongly recommend that you follow this process frequently to maintain the focus and capitalise on the momentum.

Strategic: Finally, when you employ a strategic leadership approach, your objectives have a long-term focus, relating to company strategy with people UNITED in working toward common goals. Measuring performance against the objectives is vital, firstly to know if you have achieved the objective, and secondly to know if it was worthwhile, i.e. measure the benefit.

It is at this point that you and your team leaders will restart the whole process by setting new objectives for the next period.

A quick look at objectives

Successful businesses set some form of target each year, whether it be for turnover, profit, or growth. When a business seeks certification to quality management standard ISO 9001, they must also set quality objectives as illustrated in Figure 6. This raises several questions. Should these objectives be set using the same annual process as business objectives? Are they one and the same? Innovative and market leading companies develop their quality objectives in line with the organisation's strategic priorities. No matter the industry or the organisation, or if we are talking quality or health and safety, there is one constant. Whatever your objectives, they should never be "set and forget".

Over the years I have seen many variations on objectives across many industries and businesses big and small. Interestingly, it is not always the bigger companies that have the most meaningful quality objectives. Let's explore some of the usual suspects.

Occasionally companies list their quality objectives in their Quality Policy. This might be generic statements such as "happy customers" or "consistently deliver high quality product/service". Some are more specific such as "right first time every time" or DIFOT – deliver in full on time.

What is wrong with this? To answer that, let's take a quick look at ISO9001. According to the standard, objectives need to be relevant, measurable, planned and updated. This is illustrated below in Figure 6.

Figure 6

Many will have heard of SMART objectives. The *Specific-Measurable-Achievable-Relevant-Timed* acronym remains a very helpful reference when setting objectives today.

So, let's look at "happy customers". It's not wrong, but it's not specific to what you do. Can you define happy? Would a happy customer mean there are no returns, service calls or rework? How are you going to measure "happy customers" and what is your real target? Is it 0 returns or is it 10% less returns than last year? And how are you planning to achieve this? Who is responsible for it? And how often will you be monitoring it?

Let's say you rewrite this as "Reduce returns (or rework) by 10% by 30 June" and plan a new process to reduce errors. If you then achieve that by December, does that allow you to relax for the next 6 months? What if you achieve a reduction of 15%? Do you keep the same objective again for next year? Many companies do. However, the last point in figure 6 above: 'Updated' requires you to update your objectives. If you have reached perfection then perhaps you could move to "Maintain returns/rework at less than x", but is that really inspiring anyone?

Your business may always have financial goals, and good businesses reset these each year. A quality business also goes through the same process with their quality objectives, reviewing if they've hit their targets, and setting new ones for the next year.

Ownership

The biggest challenge with objectives is how to ensure there is ownership for achieving them. This is best achieved by involving the teams in setting the direction in the first place.

For your people to take ownership of what needs to happen, they need to understand their organisation's or team's current priorities, and be involved in setting their own objectives and deciding the best actions they can take.

> Recently I was brought in to help an organisation with their strategic planning, as the manager had created a wonderful strategy document but had gained little traction from his team.
>
> There was nothing wrong with the strategic plan he had documented, nor the tactics he had cascading within it. However, there was a problem with its implementation, which boiled down to the fact that his team didn't own it.

A 2021 *Gallup* study estimates that low employee engagement costs the global economy $8.1 trillion. But it's not just profit that's impacted by low employee engagement — it's also productivity, innovation and organisational change such as staff retention.

Of course, I am not suggesting that everyone be involved in every decision made in an organisation, but I am suggesting that teams at each level be involved in determining the tactics required to deliver the strategic priorities set by leadership.

Be clear on expectations

Clear objectives established by the team help staff prioritise their daily activities and focus their efforts on working toward the goals. Regular check-ins with those objectives should reward wins and address the challenges that can stall progress on an objective.

Defined boundaries create autonomy where people understand what's expected of them and don't need to be micro-managed. Organisational charts and position contracts might at first feel tedious but as Michael Gerber tells us in the *E-myth Revisited*, they are part of the organisational strategy, essential tools for clarifying roles, responsibilities and accountabilities.

Plenty of organisations have strategy days that may be very inspiring, but successful strategy days have employees walking away with clarity of ownership on how to deliver on that strategy. The excellent ones implement a process for routinely following up the objectives, usually on a quarterly basis.

Ordinary or Excellent?

- Do you have position descriptions signed by employees?

  ____

- Are expectations regularly discussed?

  ____

- When setting objectives are staff at various levels actively involved?

  ____

- Is ownership a problem in your organisation?

  ____

Excellent organisations know that a good process for following up on objectives is essential.

Online references:

1. https://www.drkellywindle.com/
2. https://www.mckinsey.com/business-functions/people-and-organizational-performance/our-insights/help-your-employees-find-purpose-or-watch-them-leave
3. https://www.mckinsey.com/business-functions/strategy-and-corporate-finance/our-insights/the-role-of-esg-and-purpose
4. https://builtin.com/company-culture/company-culture-statistics
5. https://hbr.org/2015/12/engaging-your-employees-is-good-but-dont-stop-there

Books mentioned:

1. Collins, Jim 2001 – *Good to Great*
2. Brown, Brene 2018 – *Dare to Lead*
3. Gallup 2021 – *State of the Global Workplace 2021 Report*
4. Gerber, Michael E. 1995 – *The E Myth Revisited*

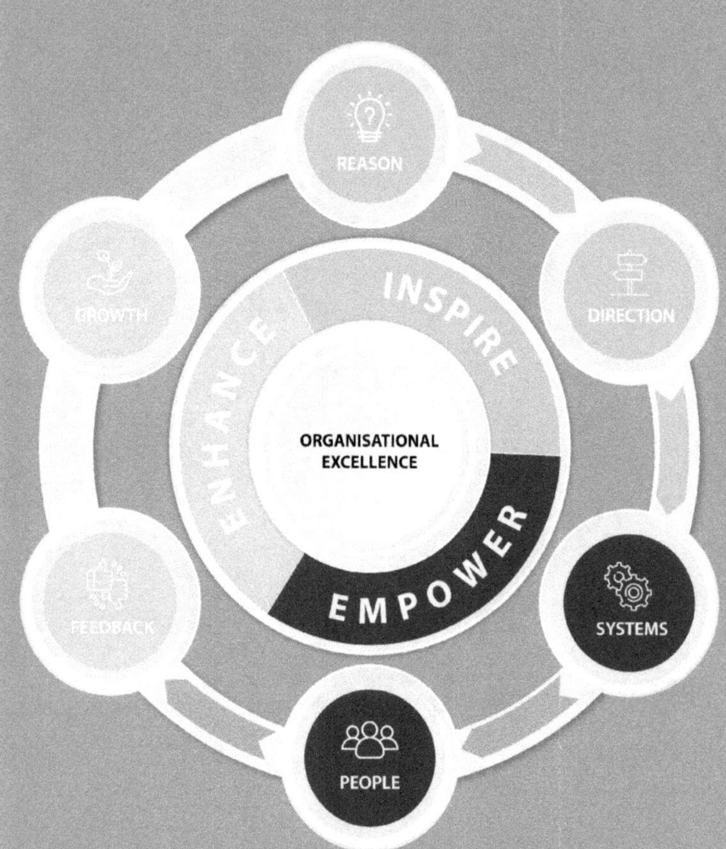

REASON
GROWTH
DIRECTION
INSPIRE
ENHANCE
ORGANISATIONAL EXCELLENCE
EMPOWER
FEEDBACK
SYSTEMS
PEOPLE

Part 2

Empower

"Investing in management means building communication systems, business processes, feedback, and routines that let you scale the business and team as efficiently as possible."

– Fred Wilson, Venture Capitalist

The second segment of the Organisational Excellence wheel is all about empowering your people. Your people are your organisation. Yet they are at times limited by systems that slow them down, sometimes through a lack of skills, and other times through a lack of opportunity. Empower your people to deliver company objectives by giving them the best systems available and increasing their individual and collective capability through training and development opportunities.

Remove obstacles

How bad were online meetings back in 2019? Back then, we thought they were pretty good actually, but the pandemic that hit in 2020 forced a big proportion of the world to work from home, and very quickly technology came ahead in leaps and bounds to meet demand. Now we have very high expectations for the ability to effectively hold meetings between remote workers, and hybrid meetings (combining in-person with remote) are to here to stay.

The simplest way to empower your people is to remove the obstacles that prevent them from doing their best. Obstacles may come in the form of poor processes with too much 'red tape', they could be stifling organisational structures, old-fashioned rules because 'that's how we've always done it', software that hasn't been upgraded, or machinery and equipment that spends more time being repaired than operating.

Organisational capability comes from tools and equipment, systems and processes, training and experience, structure and opportunity.

Back in 2016 I worked with the management of a security business to introduce quality and WHS management systems. I was shocked to hear that they wouldn't allow their technicians to use the toll roads, because management felt it cost too much.

What a poor attitude to business – avoiding a tax-deductible expense but ignoring the cost of the technicians' un-productive time spent on the road. That decision was actively creating an obstacle to hamper their technician's productivity.

Systems

Good systems allow teams to work effectively and efficiently, and to optimise productivity.

> *"85% reasons for failure are deficiencies in processes and systems rather than the employee."*
>
> – Deming

Make it easy

Sydneysiders missed the ski season in 2021 due to lockdown, but the ski slopes are beautiful in summer too.

Some years ago, we holidayed in summer at the NSW ski resort town of Perisher. There was no snow, just beautiful walks and scenery, and peace and quiet. We took the kids to the Perisher Front Valley which in a normal winter is packed with skiers learning to ski and others taking off for more adventurous ski runs in adjoining valleys.

That summer, faced with a big grassy hill, the kids did what all children do. They started to run up. They soon slowed to a walking pace, and at the first crest about a quarter of the way up, they stopped. After a quick frolic at that height, they linked arms and ran back down singing and having a ball.

The next winter we returned to this beautiful place excited to be able to take the kids skiing this time. What a different experience they had. We booked them into ski school as we didn't have the expertise to teach them well, and it freed us up to concentrate on our own skiing for a short time.

This time, instead of having to walk up Front Valley, the kids were able to start on the 'magic carpet' that pulls them up a short way to practice their skills. By the time they had completed a day of lessons they could take the chairlift to the top of the mountain and ski down from the top. My heart was in my mouth when I saw it, but they were very capable because they had been taught well and had practiced on the shorter lifts first.

I don't know how many times they went up on the chairlift and back down, but I do believe they "got their money's worth" as we say in our family.

Make it easy for your business "family" by implementing systems that take away the effort of climbing the hills and allow your team to focus on developing their performance in the areas that deliver excellence.

Ordinary or Excellent?

- Does your organisation have a 'chairlift' to take your people to the top of the mountain or are you happy to let them walk and puff out part way?

____

- Have you given them the skills to ski down when they get to the top or are you risking a crash?

____

- Are you measuring how well your team skis the mountain to "get your money's worth"?

____

- Give your team the right systems, skills and opportunities, and they'll be grinning with exhilaration.

____

Embrace Technology

"You do not rise to the level of your goals. You fall to the level of your systems."

– James Clear, Atomic Habits

Systems can come in the form of hardware and software. When they are troublesome and complicated, the systems tend to be limiting. But the right systems for an organisation can elevate your people to work to their best ability.

A 2022 *McKinsey* report on data driven organisations tells us that by 2025, smart workflows and seamless interactions among humans and machines will likely be as standard as the corporate balance sheet, and most employees will use data to optimise nearly every aspect of their work.

It warns us that if an organisation is only sporadically using predictive systems and AI-driven automation they are possibly leaving value on the table.

The report goes on to say that organisations are capable of better decision making as well as automating basic day-to-day activities and regularly occurring decisions. Employees are free to focus on more "human" domains, such as innovation, collaboration and communication. Data-driven culture fosters continuous performance improvement to create truly differentiated customer and employee experiences and to enable the growth of sophisticated new applications that aren't widely available today.

The use of technology can make the difference between a challenging work environment and engaged and effective teams. A business I once encountered invested in a lot of second-hand plant and equipment, but then had to hire a mechanic to perform all the repairs and maintenance! They avoided upfront cost only to pay for it many times over in an additional salary.

Another organisation I worked with were happy to purchase a $60,000 piece of machinery but wouldn't pay a much smaller amount for a software upgrade. They were undervaluing the role the software played in the organisation's management of quotes and jobs. By not upgrading, they were missing out on chances to improve their workflows and potentially save time by reducing the costs of doing business.

When technology is used well it should enhance the employee and customer experience, making the job easier and more satisfying. If technology is causing frustration this is a signal that it might be time to upgrade or update.

Ordinary or Excellent?

- What technology would make your job easier?

  ____

- Where is technology holding you back?

  ____

- What technology do you envision will require updating or replacing in the next 1 year / 3-5 years?

  ____

- Do you have a clear understanding of your technology assets?

Processes

Processes are the steps taken to get things done. When processes are optimised in an organisation, this allows for innovation whilst effectively controlling quality and safety, and efficiently delivering productivity.

Design your shortcut

There are a multitude of process improvement methodologies, focusing on improving quality and productivity. Back in the 1990s, as a young graduate starting out in the petrochemical industry, I was exposed to the TQM (Total Quality Management) methodology which had a strong focus on customers. Since then, I have learned about Lean, Six Sigma and their variations. The Manufacturing Industry tends to embrace productivity and process improvement the most, but no matter what industry, an understanding of the organisation's processes is *essential* to optimising them.

In early 2022 I worked with an organisation in the communications space helping them understand their key processes. We were able to identify significant steps in their processes that were causing delays due to the manual activities involved. By better understanding their compliance requirements and introducing some automation, they were able to remove the most laborious steps from these processes. The benefit was realised when - through natural attrition - they were able to reduce the administrative overhead. A staff member left, and they didn't have to replace them.

Understanding the steps required to get the results you want will help you finetune your processes to increase efficiency and productivity. It will also ensure everyone is aware of the optimal process to deliver consistency in your product or service.

Conduct regular reviews of your processes to look for opportunities for automation and better ways of doing things. You might find a cumbersome step was introduced long ago by a customer need, that is no longer relevant, or a process is followed because "that's the way it is always done". Too often, the people following these processes don't understand why. A review can clarify requirements and remove unnecessary and often time-consuming activities.

Ordinary or Excellent?

- Have you mapped your key processes?

  ____

- Do you understand the costs of each step?

  ____

- Are your processes optimised?

  ____

- Do people take 'shortcuts' that are not approved?

  ____

- Are your processes automated wherever possible?

  ____

- What processes could be automated now or in the next 1-3 years?

  ____

People

Raise the capability of your organisation by ensuring your people are skilled and continually expanding these skills. If everyone is aiming to be just 10% better each year, your organisational growth will be exponential.

Let them grow

Have you watched any of the Spiderman movies or even read the comics? You might recall that teenager Peter Parker is in a laboratory when he is bitten by a radioactive spider. He somehow gains superhuman strength, speed and agility, and he develops the ability to shoot webs. But he's a teenager, so he not only has to learn how to control his web shooting and his speed, he must learn to make the right choices around how he will use his newfound powers.

Part of the appeal of the movie is watching the personal journey Peter goes on as he transitions from a typical teenager to become Spiderman.

How many superheroes are hiding in your organisation?

Trusting your people to learn and develop their skills will ensure they are fulfilled at work. You will see them grow professionally and uncover a few secret superpowers along the way. The result is higher performance because you are allowing your people to perform at their best to work in your organisation.

Selection

People are the heart of any organisation. It's not always easy selecting the right people for your organisation, and even harder to shed the wrong ones.

The right people on the bus

In his book *Good to Great*, Jim Collins talks about getting the "right people on the bus and the wrong people off".

Organisational Excellence requires people who not only have skills that will complement the team, but who challenge the current mix i.e. people who have the ability to grow, and who can take your organisation into the future.

Did Ash Barty really win the Australian Open in 2022? If you listen carefully to her speeches and media answers, it was Team Barty who won, not just the individual. She was the player on the court, but it was the combination of an excellent team executing their strategy that delivered the results.

Ash Barty has been a good tennis player for a long time, but in 2015 she took a break to be a normal teenager for a while, to play cricket and decide what she wanted to commit to.

On returning to the professional tennis circuit in 2016 she formed a team that comprised coach, manager, mindset coach, trainers and physiotherapist.

"We're all equal," Barty said of her team.

"We all play our roles, and the most amazing thing is we all communicate really well together and get along with each other and know when it's time to back off and relax, and then when it's time to switch on and really have a crack."

What are you hiring for?

A 2020 *Gartner* report (28 September 2020) suggests leaders should focus on shaping the workforce, not replacing them. This report was further analysed by *Harvard Business Review* in 2022 suggesting that hiring leaders should look beyond the current needs of the business and think about what skills the organisation might need going into the future.

If you are aiming to take your ordinary organisation on a journey towards excellence, you need a team who are prepared to grow with you. You need people who bring skills that will help deliver your purpose and who have a growth mindset – people who are comfortable learning and able to try new things. An ideal mix would be someone who is innovative and yet quick to admit when they're wrong and comfortable seeking advice from best practice.

Development

Organisational capability is expanded by developing the right skills across the organisation so that leaders at all levels are empowered.

> *"Happy employees lead to happy customers, which leads to more profits."*
>
> – Vaughn Aust, EVP of Integrated Solutions, MarketStar

As a young leader (and even as an older one) I sometimes have struggled with 'letting go'. Have you ever been caught saying "It's quicker if I do it myself" or "It'll be done properly if I just do it myself"? However you are not empowering your team when you try to do everything yourself.

At some time, there will come a tipping point where you just can't do everything yourself, and you will have to delegate to others. If you have given them opportunities along the way, your team are more likely to be able to easily step up when needed.

When delegating it should be seen as a learning experience and come with a level of coaching to do the job well. Therein lies the rub – how to tread the fine line between supervising and giving them the freedom to work it out for themselves. This is where managers often find it quicker to do it themselves and 'get it right'.

However, this is a very short term view towards your team's development and yours. When individuals in your team grow, you can all benefit as the workload shifts, and their ability to take on more responsibility can raise your overall team performance.

Next time question if it really is "quicker if I do it myself".

Invest in your team

Forbes HR Council (Forbes Magazine 17 December 2021) talks about the 16 Benefits of Training and Development, including lower turnover rates, attraction of new candidates, employee self-initiative and growth, preparing a stronger workforce, and contribution to team success. This is backed up by data from the US National Center for the Middle Market showing clear correlation between superior talent planning and company performance.

If you have a hands-on, practical workforce then of course they must be skilled in the tasks they are expected to carry out. But are you also giving them the opportunity to develop leadership and problem-solving skills?

Excellent organisations have people across all levels of the organisation who are skilled in leadership and problem solving.

Stop fighting fires

What a dramatic few weeks we had on the east coast of Australia at the end of summer 2022! Traumatic, destructive and tragic, and just downright dramatic. (For those not based here, we saw repeated east coast low pressure systems bring deluges of rain for weeks on end, causing record-breaking flood levels in many areas).

Australians, like many other people, love an emergency. Communities rally together to help each other through, and SES volunteers and professionals turn up to coordinate rescue and relief efforts. Then the people hit hardest by the disaster are interviewed on TV and they smile through tears, buoyed by the generosity of others showing gratitude to be alive.

But I noticed something a little different in this natural disaster: People were complaining. Only one person on TV spoke with any gratitude and my daughter suggested they were being sarcastic.

Could it be that it is all too much too soon? We had major flooding last year too, and horrific bushfires the year before, all occurring with a pandemic in the background. There are suggestions that in some areas, the emergency systems in place were ineffective due to the unexpected scale of the emergency.

These events are real, but they also act as an analogy for business. When I think back to my manufacturing days, it was most exciting when things went wrong. There were a few heroes in the business who would come in and save the day. Their trouble-shooting skills went so far as addressing the failure in the moment, but only when a structured problem-solving approach was followed could we eliminate the problem long term.

Looking at the floods, the heroes were rescuing trapped people, doing food drops to isolated areas and helping with clean up and eventually repair. These people need to be thanked, but there is another set of heroes who need to look into prevention, and to do that they need to get to the real cause. Was it building on a flood plain, was it overpopulation, poor planning or climate change that caused this natural disaster? Depending on the answers, the solutions will vary.

Of course we won't stop fighting fires or rescuing people in need, but we can make sure the heroes in our business are not only the "fire-fighters" but also the solvers.

Problem solving and innovation

You may ask what does problem-solving have to do with innovation. It is stated that most people prefer either logical or intuitive thinking, and people often describe themselves as one or the other. But this can be self-limiting. The reality is most of us are a bit of both. Engineers who love maths might be thought of as logical thinkers, but dig deeper and we find they are also quite creative people, responsible for building bridges, tunnels, aircraft, software programs, etc.

Excellent organisations get to the cause.

Increasingly, universities are recognising the need for people to have a broader approach to innovation and are introducing all types of thinking in their bachelor degrees now. The older universities still teach Lean Six Sigma which is an important, disciplined, data and statistical analysis tool, but the younger universities are putting poets with scientists to develop broader thinking styles in their graduates. For example, you've probably heard of de Bono's Six Thinking Hats, in use since 1985, a method which uses diverse perspectives to encourage creativity to a problem or an innovation.

So, is problem-solving the same as innovation? By training your teams and encouraging the use of various types of thinking when approaching non-conformances or incidents, the solutions can be innovative and your business will reap the rewards.

Leadership can be learned

There is an old argument about whether people are natural leaders or if leadership can be learned. Through years of observation of my colleagues, clients and myself, I believe that the answer lies neatly in between.

Of course, there are natural leaders, but they can perform badly if the conditions don't suit them. The smartest leaders learn leadership styles and techniques to use in different situations that enhance their natural ability. And then there are those closet leaders, who are too afraid to step into their abilities - but

Occasionally a leader needs to look in the mirror to see how well they are doing.

when given a chance - are able to explore their strengths and demonstrate leadership.

Forbes Magazine (2021) tells us that leaders can perform better through coaching, 360° feedback and personality assessments, and by boosting leaders' knowledge and expertise. It warns that those most amenable to improving their leadership skills may need it the least, however I believe this gives the organisation the opportunity to identify their best leaders.

Do you recall "the Fonz" from Happy Days? In the opening credits there is a scene where he looks in the mirror with comb in hand, then deciding his hair is already perfect he puts the comb back in his pocket and walks out.

Occasionally a leader needs to look in the mirror to see how well they are doing and recognise where they need some help. Young people don't instantly 'know' how to shave or put on makeup or style their hair. They learn from their parents and others skilled in grooming. Young leaders who are taught and mentored in management techniques can more confidently apply them in practice in the workplace.

Ordinary or Excellent?

- Do you trust your managers?

- Do you trust your employees?

  ____

- Do you pay for development of skills?

  ____

- Are there clear career paths in your organisation?

  ____

- Have you sent staff on external training for soft skills such as leadership or problem solving?

  ____

- Is mentoring in place in your organisation?

  ____

- Do you hire people for their skills / experience / potential?

  ____

- Do you have a development program for current or aspiring leaders in your organisation?

  ____

Online references:

1. https://www.mckinsey.com/business-functions/ mckinsey-analytics/our-insights/the-data-driven- enterprise-of-2025
2. https://hbr.org/2021/03/reengineering-the-recruitment- process
3. https://hbr.org/2021/03/reengineering-the-recruitment- process
4. https://www.forbes.com/sites/ forbeshumanresourcescouncil/2021/12/17/ hr-experts-explain-16-benefits-of-training-and- development/?sh=1f7d92007d1e
5. https://hbr.org/2021/07/leadership-training-can-pay- huge-dividends-for-midsize-companies

Books mentioned:

1. Collins, Jim 2001 – *Good to Great*
2. *Forbes Magazine* 17 December 2021
3. Clear, James 2018 – *Atomic Habits*

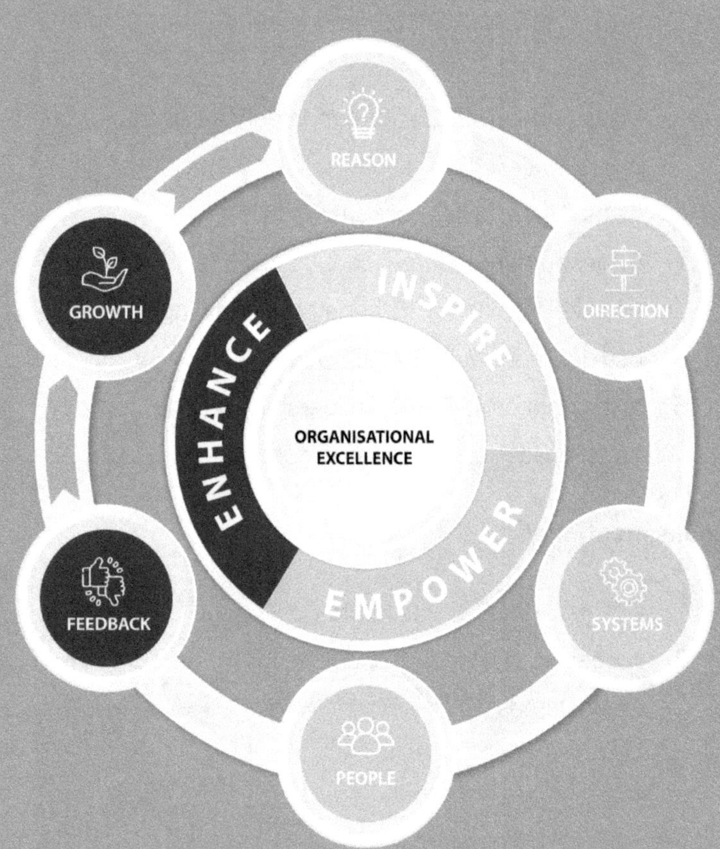
REASON
DIRECTION
GROWTH
SYSTEMS
FEEDBACK
PEOPLE
ENHANCE
INSPIRE
EMPOWER
ORGANISATIONAL EXCELLENCE

Part 3

Enhance

"Excellent firms don't believe in excellence – only in constant improvement and constant change."

– Tom Peters, Consultant and Author

The third element of the organisational excellence cycle is enhancing your processes and business performance. It's about monitoring success and failure with the aim of refining what you do, how you do it and enhancing the results.

Tirelessly tweak

At this point I am going to admit something which may contradict my mantra stated throughout this book regarding Organisational Excellence.

You may never quite achieve "excellence".

You might be very close but then something changes. A senior partner moves on, technological advances completely change the market, a global pandemic hits - you get the picture.

This shouldn't stop you *trying*. In fact, it is the ability to observe these changes and be able to adapt to them that will allow your company to survive. Staying ahead of the competition by minimising costs and maximising service will give you the edge needed to be an enduring organisation.

And what about the "boring" times? When we are doing the same thing year on year without too much change, we can become complacent. This is also the time to keep improving and growing – enhancing your business performance - striving to do better and better in every area of the business.

But you can't do better if you don't know how well you are doing.

We are taught that in relationships we shouldn't keep score, and I would agree. However, to enhance your business requires measurement, and understanding of *which* measures are important.

> *"However beautiful the strategy, you should occasionally look at the results."*
> – Sir Winston Churchill

Sports teams review their performance at half time, to make adjustments in the second half. At the end of the match, they know where they are on the leader board and use that information to plan for the next match against the upcoming opponent.

Similarly, organisations that "keep score" find it easier to know which areas to focus on for continual improvement programs. In *Good to Great*, Jim Collins talks about 'Great' organisations finding what they do well and then continually improving on it.

A 2018 *Harvard Business* study of seven 100-year-old organisations talks about British Cycling making 1000 x 1% tweaks to deliver a 1000% improvement.

A structured continual improvement program that is understood across the organisation builds a culture of contribution where workers at all levels are thinking about better ways of doing things.

The score is not something to fear, rather it can be a catalyst for working together to improve results for everyone.

Ordinary or Excellent?

- Are your customers blown away by the service you deliver? How do you know?

____

- Do your employees love their job? Are they as productive as they can be?

____

- Is waste measured in your company? What about productivity? Or rework?

____

- What measure is most important to your organisations' success?

____

Feedback

Seeking and assessing feedback is essential to provide key measures on performance of internal processes as well as final output.

Seek to understand

Do you ever feel like you or your business has a case of the wobbles? Turns out it might not be such a bad thing.

> Recently my Pilates instructor told me not to stop an exercise when I get the wobbles. Rather the wobbles were just an indication that my body had to learn to activate some of the lesser used muscles to work harder to retain balance. I was too reliant on the same old muscles and some unused muscles needed to be switched on.

If your business does have a case of the wobbles, it's not necessarily a sign that you must stop what you are doing. Rather it is time to learn from what's not going right, improve your processes, involve the right people, and maybe even empower others to step up to do their bit.

The important lesson here is that the wobbles is a form of feedback. If we ignore it, we may never be able to complete the exercise successfully. As a business leader it is not easy being told that something isn't going right, or that we need to improve our people skills or project management skills or perhaps our strategic plans for the business.

Having a regular review process or 'check-in' in any of these areas will help you respond to the wobbles before you 'fall over', and to 'activate the lesser used muscles' in your business. Check-ins are used extensively in high performing businesses, for example in the team objectives process, in staff one-on-ones, and in leadership coaching.

Is your business utilizing check-ins to seek feedback and manage the wobbles?

Keep Score

The challenge can be identifying the right things to measure and how to communicate them.

"If you can't read the scoreboard, you don't know the score. If you don't know the score, you can't tell the winners from the losers."

– Warren Buffett

Organisational Excellence is not an end game, rather it's a journey a business travels on that consists of continually enhancing business processes and the services or products delivered.

Do you understand you core business? What is it that your business does? Have you improved how you do that over time?

Let me pose another question to you – how do you know you've improved? So, for example, you've implemented that new software. Great, what did that improve?

To enhance a business' performance, you need to be measuring it. There will be a few key pieces of data that will tell you how well you are doing. Profitability might seem obvious, but some measure revenue. They often relate but they are not the same thing.

You might also measure employee engagement. This can be through staff turnover, productivity and efficiency rates, or survey results. I'm not going to tell you what your business needs to measure, but I will suggest that if you have identified a problem or an area that you would like to improve, then you need to measure it to have an idea where you are starting from.

Perhaps you don't have any problems. You've been running this business for years and it's going really well. This is the time to Enhance. I'm not talking radical change, I'm talking about the fine tuning on what is already working. The old saying goes "if it ain't broke don't fix it". But the world is continually changing, people move on, technology advances, and competitors rise and fall.

I'm not saying you need to change the way you do business, just be prepared to do a little enhancing to get you up the next hill.

Measure cause and effect

There is a place for both lead and lag indicators, particularly in the area of safety. Focusing on one without the other doesn't give the whole picture.

Which soccer team is better? The one who has 20 shots at the goal, but is shut down by strong defence, or the one who defends well and then makes a breakaway goal.

Watching the Matildas vs the Ferns in April 2022, the Matildas looked the strongest team all the way through. They dominated and had the ball up the near the goal for most of the match, yet they weren't able to execute. Then late in the first half, the Ferns made a break and were able to score, holding the lead at 1-0 until the final minutes of the game.

In those exhilarating final few minutes, the Matildas managed to even the score and then continue to shoot a winning goal in the final seconds!

If the Matildas had only evened the score, which team would have been judged the strongest? Analysis of that match is not only about the goals, but also the setups, the mistakes, the skills, the teamwork and the plays, because the Matildas are not only about one goal, and they're not only out to win one match.

Do you measure setups and plays, skills and teamwork?

Review

Build in regular processes to make it normal to seek, give and receive feedback.

> *"Make feedback normal. Not a performance review."*
> – Ed Batista

Every sports team checks the score at half-time and again at the end of the game. Work teams should also be keen to know how they are performing. Performance targets don't need to be secret, in fact they should be a comfortable and routine discussion. Manufacturers count how many widgets they produce each day. Project managers count if the project is on time and budget. Sales teams count the items sold.

It's the trickier or non-routine performance measures that are less routinely reviewed and sometimes altogether forgotten. But the answer is simple. If you set annual objectives and targets, also set a review process and make it no less frequent that quarterly. Any longer than that and you haven't been working on the objective.

Normalise feedback – embrace the hecklers

My neighbour told me his story recently. What you need to know about him is that he's the type of guy who stands up and gets involved. He used to run his own marketing agency but when an opportunity arose with a big client of his, a well-known pharmaceutical company, he took the job. After working there for several years, a new manager was sent from the home country, and brought with him a change in culture. My neighbour was set a "personal development objective" to "stay quiet in meetings".

That objective was effective, but it was not a development opportunity for my neighbour. He told me that he instantly stopped caring. "I used to speak up because I cared" he said. Soon after he was submitting job applications elsewhere.

People usually speak up because they care. They might not always be eloquent or direct their passion where it is most useful, but this is where a skilful leader can embrace them through inclusion. Embrace the 'hecklers' by getting their support and sign-off for initiatives early.

Leaders need to be open to improving. Your team know your best and your worst. Brene Brown encourages leaders to seek feedback from the team and be open even if they're not skilled in delivering it.

Think about a stand-up comedian, the best ones don't belittle their audience, rather they build on the comments that come from the crowd. Harness your team members' passion and respond to their feedback. Don't silence it.

Ordinary or Excellent?

- Do you have a dashboard with essential performance data?

____

- Are you regularly checking-in on objectives progress?

____

- Is feedback normal or only once per year or less?

____

- How do you measure leading and lagging indicators?

  ____

- Are skills and teamwork assessed?

  ____

- What else is important to your company health?

  ____

- Could you share this data better?

  ____

Growth

Organisations not just individuals need a growth mindset to provide for both reactive and proactive improvement.

"No company can afford not to move forward. It may be at the top of the heap today but at the bottom of the heap tomorrow, if it doesn't."

– James Cash Penney, Founder, JC Penney

Better not bigger

Do you have a garden? Every gardener knows that a beautiful garden is the result of constant tending and continual improvement. It requires weeding, pruning, some seasonal planting, and occasionally moving plants to a better location, or even replacing them with a different variety.

In 2018, the *Harvard Business Review* published the results of a 5-year study on 100-year-old organisations which was conducted to understand the secrets to their successful longevity. A number of findings stood out to me, but none more so than the focus on "better not bigger". The authors of the study talk about "a stable core and a disruptive edge", stating that these organisations "tirelessly tweak" to make many small improvements rather than implement any monumental or disruptive changes.

Companies with ISO 9001 certification will be familiar with the concept of continual improvement. The 100-year-old organisations in the study included NASA, Eton College, the New Zealand All Blacks, and the Royal Academy of Music. They are leading examples of the ISO 9001 continual improvement process – they have a stable purpose, yet they continually seek to improve.

Perhaps you've visited the Royal Botanic Gardens in Sydney recently. It is a glorious wonder and is over 200 years old. Next time you wander through, take a moment to notice that the gardens are also being tirelessly tweaked and the result of continual improvement.

Ordinary or Excellent?

- Does your organisation have a growth mindset?

  ____

- Are you routinely looking to enhance your product or service?

  ____

> - Do you have a training & development plan for the organisation?

Reactive Change

To manage reactive change requires skilful use of incident investigation and problem-solving techniques.

Get to the source

Do you have productivity issues in your business? Are customer complaints or returns common? Are there known problems that repeatedly raise their ugly head, causing delays and frustration? Are people being injured?

Many companies have an 'issue' log which is used to capture recurring problems or "incidents", and assign an owner to investigate the root cause, to prevent it from recurring. However, all too often the person responsible has no training in any form of root cause analysis. Assuming they can find the root cause(s), often the corrective actions put in place may not resolve the issue permanently.

It is important that the people responsible for managing this process have the skills to prioritise and investigate, and/or the authority to delegate. The focus must be on resolving problems not just making them go away.

When there is an overload of problems to fix, the 'fire-fighting' approach that ensues can result in poor investigation and temporary patching. To help through these times Roger Bohn from the University of California suggests 3 approaches:

1. bring in more resources to assist with investigation
2. triage or prioritise the problems (and admit some won't be resolved)
3. shut down operations until things are under control

Management needs to understand the size of the problem and act quickly to allocate resources appropriately. This is the approach for a major safety incident and should be the same for a major quality incident too.

Ordinary or Excellent?

- Are your people trained in problem-solving?

  ____

- Do you log quality problems?

  ____

- Have you ever brought in external help with investigations?

  ____

- Are you able to identify higher value (cost) problems?

Proactive Improvement

Organisational Excellence requires a continual improvement program for proactively resolving issues and consciously looking to improve processes.

> *"They always say time changes things, but you actually have to change them yourself."*
>
> – Andy Warhol, Artist

Assess the risk

Continual Improvement is not just about ticking things off your wish list or improving something because you think it might be better. Proactive continual improvement is most effective when a structured approach is used.

First identify the cost (or risk) of each problem on your improvement list. It's hard to measure if you have made an improvement, unless you understand where you are starting from and determine if the benefit is worth the effort that change requires.

We often think of proactive improvements in terms of productivity, but you might also consider measuring internal frustration levels, customer complaints, waste, injuries, or other incidents. Ultimately all of these can impact profitability.

Once you understand the cost of the problem, conduct a first pass prioritisation of your improvement projects.

The next step then is to use structured problem-solving techniques to define the problem and identify relevant solutions, which are then passed through a second prioritisation based on the cost and benefit of the change.

There are a number of structured problem-solving techniques. A good one is the S.O.L.V.E framework as described in Ishan Galapathy's book *Advance*, where V stands for Validate. This is done through monitoring and data collection and by quantifying the savings or improvements made.

Conscious improvement

An Improvement Wishlist is not a bad thing. It's a great starting point, and with a bit of data to back it up, it can help you make a difference to the bottom line.

Excellent organisations measure the cost of the problem.

Immediately after winning the Australian Open in 2022, Ash Barty said she was 'getting better and better'. (This was before she subsequently shocked the world by announcing her retirement).

The Barty strategy had been continual improvement - not just to win matches, but to work on her game until she was good on every court surface, to then continue to work on her game even more. If you watched her back in 2019 you could be forgiven for thinking that her World No 1 title might have been short-lived, but she didn't rest on her laurels. She and her team fine-tuned her strengths and reduced her weaknesses resulting in a Wimbledon win followed by an Australian Open campaign where she didn't drop a set and made history by being the first Aussie to win in 44 years!

Your organisation might not be trying to make history, but with the right team and a strategy of continual improvement you might start winning some matches.

Ordinary or Excellent?

- Do you have a formal enterprise risk assessment process?

  ____

- Are projects risks assessed and documented?

  ____

- Do you have improvement teams?

  ____

- Are results of improvement projects measured?

  ____

- Do you use a structured approach to continual improvement?

  ____

Online references:

1. https://hbr.org/2018/09/how-winning-organizations-last-100-years
2. https://hbr.org/2000/07/stop-fighting-fires

Books mentioned:

1. Brown, Brene 2018 – *Dare to Lead*
2. de Bono, Edward 1985 – *Six Thinking Hats*
3. Galapathy, Ishan 2021 – *Advance*

Conclusion

"Strive for continuous improvement, instead of perfection."

– Kim Collins, World Champion 100m Sprinter

If you continually strive to be 10% better, if you follow the simple Inspire-Empower-Enhance cycle, then your organisation will no longer be ordinary.

You will be on the road to Excellence.

There are a lot of ordinary organisations in the world. And many of them will do ok, for a while. But every now and then you come across one where the people are inspired by the leadership and are following the same dreams. Where they are empowered to make things happen to achieve the company goals. Where processes are continually being refined and enhanced to adapt to market demands or the latest technology. Where profits are reinvested in the business to continue strengthening it. Where the business is leading the industry rather than just following blindly along.

Your organisation may choose to operate as a bunch of distracted individuals, harbouring frustrations at immature processes and inadequate systems. It might be tough to make ends meet at times, the business just surviving from one month to the next. This type of operation can continue for years but won't necessarily survive the curve balls that can occur such as the failure of a major client, loss of a major contract, loss of key staff or a significant change in the business environment.

There is a way to step out of the continual grind of 'ordinary' to elevate your business above the grind.

Following the Inspire – Empower – Enhance cycle will guide your organisation to continually become 10% better. By taking this path toward Organisational Excellence your people will be engaged, profits will rise, and you will build resilience and longevity so your organisation can sustain change and challenge and be a legacy into the future.